LET'S INVESTIGATE
Angles

LET'S INVESTIGATE
Angles

By Marion Smoothey

Illustrated by Ted Evans

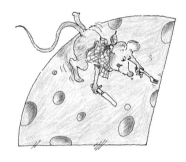

MARSHALL CAVENDISH

NEW YORK · LONDON · TORONTO · SYDNEY

Library Edition Published 1993

© Marshall Cavendish Corporation 1993

Published by Marshall Cavendish Corporation
2415 Jerusalem Avenue
PO Box 587
North Bellmore
New York 11710

Series created by Graham Beehag Book Design

Library of Congress Cataloging-in-Publication Data

Smoothey, Marion, 1943-
   Angles / by Marion Smoothey; illustrated by Ted Evans.
     p. cm.. -- (Let's Investigate)
   Includes index.
   Summary: Explores the world of angles and how they can be created, measured, and used in various activities.
   ISBN 1-85435-466-3 ISBN 1-85435-463-9 (set)
   1. Angle -- Juvenile literature.
   [1. Angle 2. Geometry.]
   I. Evans, Ted ill. II. Title. III. Series:
   Smoothey, Marion, 1943- Let's Investigate.
   QA482.S568 1993   92-36222
   516' . 15---dc20   CIP
                              AC

Printed in Singapore by Times Offset PTE Ltd
Bound in the United States

Contents

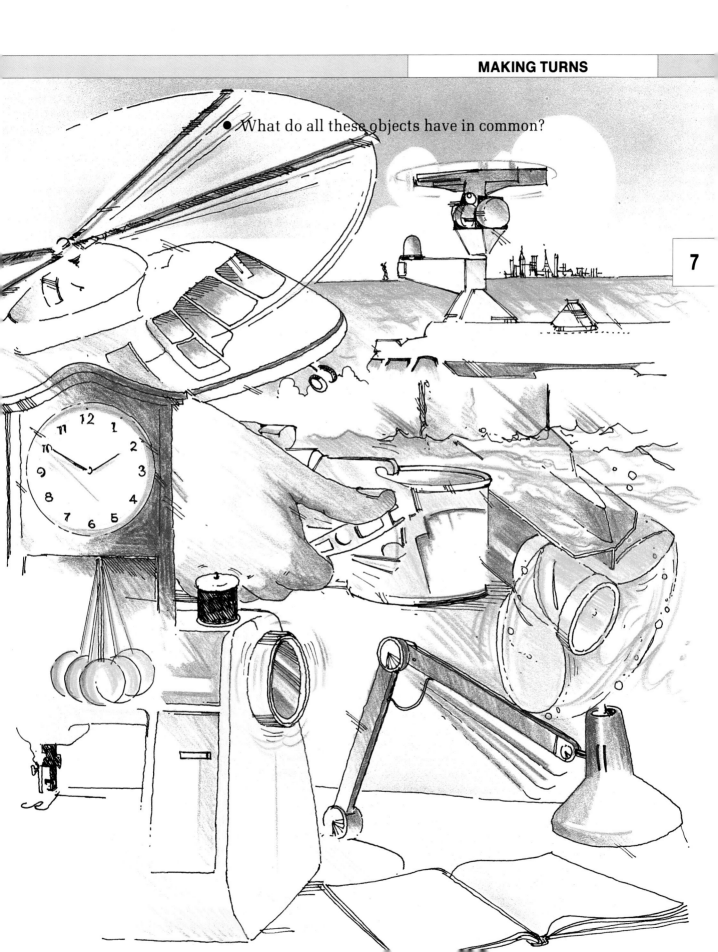

● What do all these objects have in common?

Making Turns

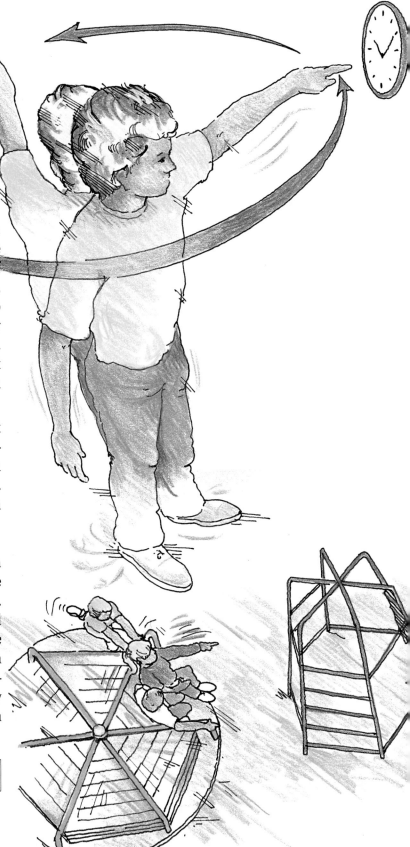

8

All the objects on page 7 can turn. You can turn as well.

1. Stand on a mark on the floor. Look at an object, such as a picture or a chair, that is straight ahead of you. Still standing on the mark, turn around to your right and keep turning clockwise, the same way as the hands move around a clock. Keep going until you are looking at the object again. Have you made a whole turn?

2. Stand on the same mark, look at the same object and turn counter-clockwise, to your left, until you are looking at the object again. How much of a turn have you made this time?

3. Adam and Beth are sitting on the merry-go-round. They can see the jungle gym straight ahead. Gary pushes the merry-go-round for them. They have seen the jungle gym straight ahead of them four more times when the merry-go-round stops again. How many turns have Adam and Beth each made?

Turn to page 10.

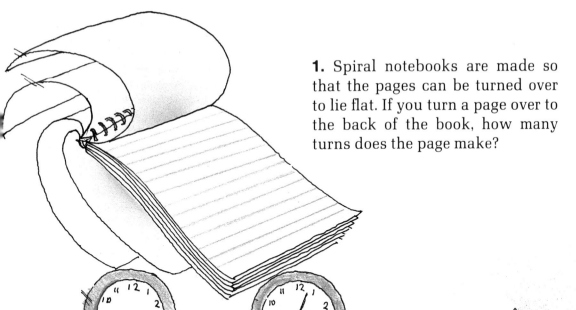

1. Spiral notebooks are made so that the pages can be turned over to lie flat. If you turn a page over to the back of the book, how many turns does the page make?

2. How many turns has the minute hand made between breakfast and lunch?

3. How many full turns will you make from the top to the bottom of this spiral slide?

**Check your answers on page 61.
If you have gotten them wrong and cannot see why, ask an adult for help. When you understand, go on to page 10.**

Answers to page 8.

1. & **2.** You turned a whole turn each time.

3. Adam and Beth each made four whole turns.

If you got these right, go on to the rest of this page. If you got any of them wrong, turn back to page 9.

10

Parts of a Turn

Some things cannot make a whole turn. They can only make part of a turn. The joints of our bones allow us to make turns with our legs, arms, hands, pelvis and so on. Some people, like dancers and athletes, train to be very agile and flexible, but we cannot make whole turns with all of our joints.

● **1.** Cuthbert Crocodile can open his mouth very wide. When his mouth is open as far as it will go, how much of a turn has his top jaw made from the bottom?

● **2.** A box can be made to open out flat. How much of a turn does the lid make?

● **3.** If you place a coin on the tray of this money box, the figure lifts the coin into its mouth. What fraction of a turn does the tray make?

● **4.** Some cars have a fold down tray in the glove compartment which is useful for holding drinks. How much of a turn does it make?

● **5.** How much of a turn does it take to turn this tap all the way on?

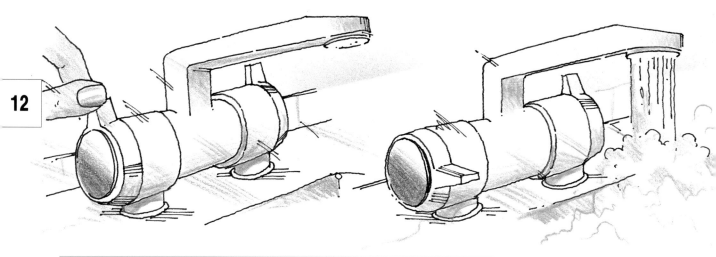

Check your answers on page 14.

When you unscrew a bottle cap or unlock a door, switch on the light or turn a handle, notice whether you are making a whole turn, less than a whole turn or more than a whole turn.

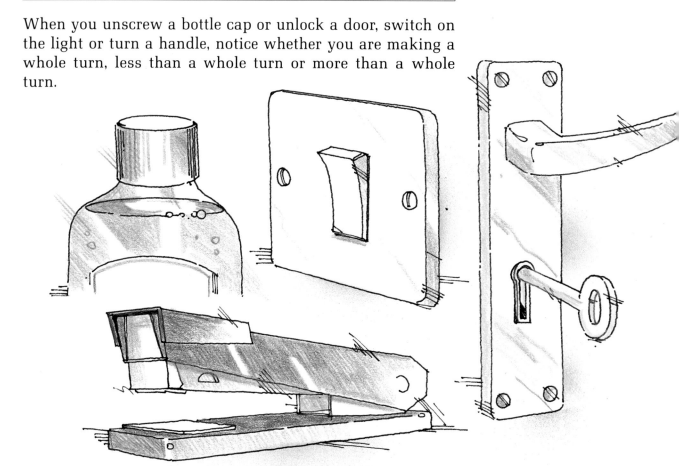

12

Semaphore

Semaphore is a way of sending messages using the angle made by your arms with your body. If you hold flags in your hands, it is easier to read but it is not essential.

You begin with both arms at your sides. The first four letters of the alphabet are made with your right arm and the next three with your left arm.

Raise your right arm an eighth of a turn. This means **A**. To make **B**, you raise your right arm a quarter turn from your side. **C** is three-eighths of a turn from your side and **D** is half a turn.

To make **E**, raise your left arm three-eighths. **F** is half a turn with the left arm, and **G** is an eighth of a turn with the left arm. The stick figures below show how it is done.

Blue = right arm
Red = left arm

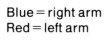

A   B   C   D   E   F   G

● Can you read these words? The figure is facing you.

● Draw a figure facing you signaling **CAB**.

For the rest of the letters you have to combine parts of turns with both arms. If you are interested in learning the rest of the alphabet, look in an encyclopedia under "semaphore."

Turn to page 16.

Answers to pages 10, 11 and 12

1. Cuthbert can open his mouth a quarter turn.
2. The lid of the box makes a half turn.
3. The tray makes a quarter turn.
4. The tray makes a half turn.
5. It takes a quarter turn to turn the tap all the way on.

14

> **If you got these all correct, turn back to page 13.**
> **If you got some wrong try the ones below.**

● **1.** Stand with your hands by your sides. Raise your right arm level with your shoulder. How much of a turn has your arm made? There are at least two ways of doing this. Is the amount of turn still the same whichever way you do it?

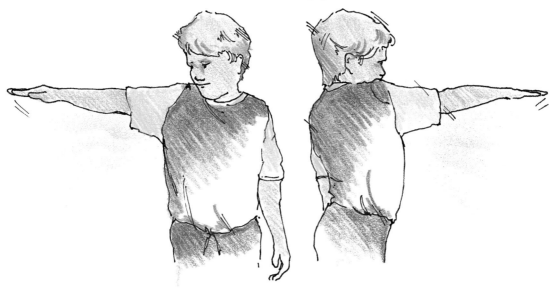

● **2.** Bring your arm back down to your side. How much of a turn has your arm made?

● **3.** Stand with your hands by your sides. Raise your left arm straight up in the air. How much of a turn has your arm made?

● **4.** Stand with your feet together. Move your right foot forward. Now, swing your right foot around to the right until it is directly behind you. How much of a turn has your right foot made?

● **5.** Stand with your arms as straight up in the air as you can. Touch your toes. How much of a turn have your arms made?

Simon Says

You can play Simon Says using instructions with turns and parts of turns. You use instructions like, Simon says, "Raise your knee a quarter turn" or Simon says, "Turn your head a half turn." Anyone who does it wrong is out and the last person to do it is out. Remember that often there is more than one way of doing it.

Turn to page 13.

Lines and Angles

Cut two strips of cardboard about $\frac{1}{2}$ inch wide and 8 inches long. Punch a hole in each strip as close to the end as possible. Fasten the strips on top of each other with a paper fastener.

Rotate the top strip to make different sized angles. Each part of a turn makes an angle between the two strips.

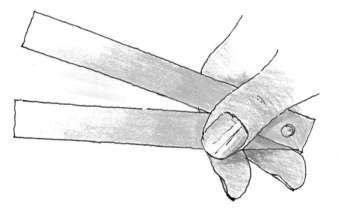

When two lines meet at a point, they make an angle. The size of the angle is the amount one line would have to turn to rest on top of the other.

If you don't have any cardboard and a paper fastener, you can use two straws or pencils. Hold their ends together with one hand and turn one of them with the other hand.

Try to rank these angles from the smallest to the largest. You can try to do it by just looking, or you can use tracing paper to help you. Trace what you think is the smallest angle and then use the tracing to compare it with the rest. Then trace what you think is the next largest angle and test it against the others. Continue making tracings until you have gotten all the angles in order.

17

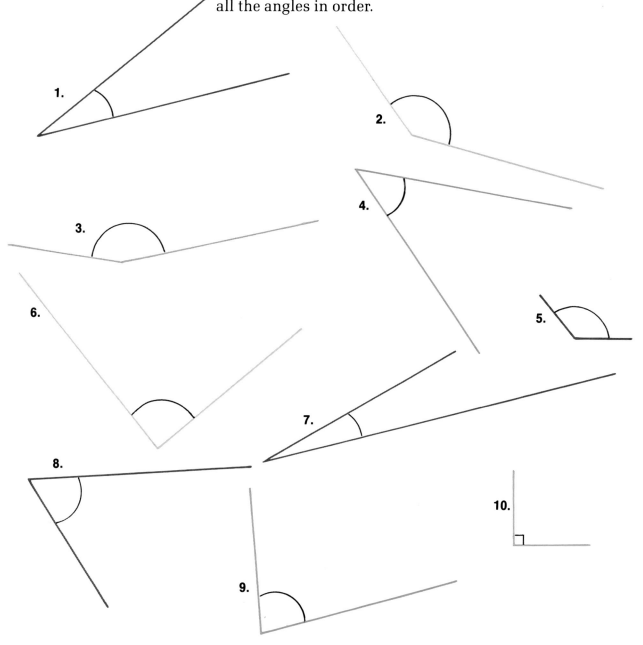

Answers to page 17

From the smallest to the largest the angles are: **7.**, **1.**, **4.**, **8.**, **9.**, **6.**, **10.**, **5.**, **2.**, **3.**

If you got any of them in the wrong order, go back and check where you went wrong. If you got them all correct, well done. You are looking at it from the right angle!

18

● It's Cuthbert's dinner time. He is very lazy; each time he eats an "angle" fish he opens his mouth just wide enough to swallow it. See if you can match the angle of Cuthbert's jaw with the "angle" fish he is about to eat.

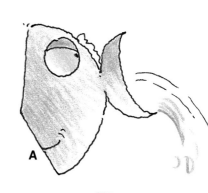

● Which of these angles are less than a quarter turn and which are more than a quarter turn?

If you need help, fold a quarter turn on tracing paper and see whether each angle is bigger, smaller or the same as a quarter turn. To fold a quarter turn, you make one fold anywhere across your paper. Then fold the fold back on itself and make another fold. Open up your paper. Where the folds cross, you have four quarter turns.

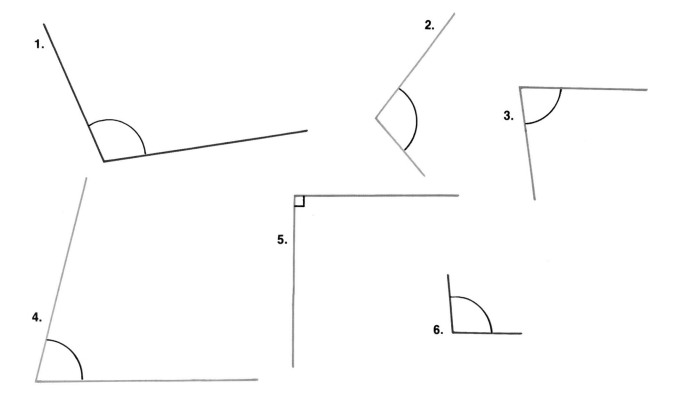

☆ **Hint:**
You can lay your tracing paper over each angle. Make sure one of the folds is exactly on top of one of the lines. If the other line is exactly under the next fold, then the angle is a quarter turn.

Answers to Cuthbert's dinner

1 and C, 2 and F, 3 and A, 4 and B, 5 and D, 6 and E.

> **If you got any wrong, go back and take another look. If you matched all the pairs correctly, well done.**

20

Tricky questions

● **1.** Which of these angles is the biggest? Which line would have to turn the most to reach its partner? If you need to, use tracing paper to help figure it out.

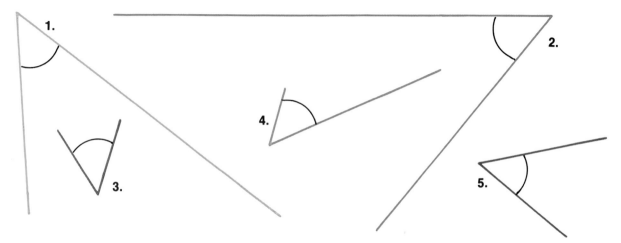

● **2.** How many quarter turns are there in each of these diagrams?

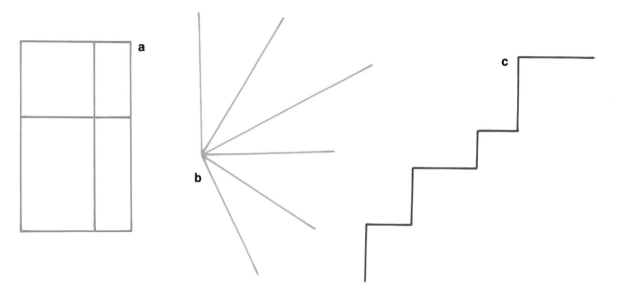

Measuring Angles in Degrees

We can measure angles. To do so, we divide one whole turn, or **revolution** into 360 degrees. The symbol for degrees is°: 360 degrees can be written as 360°.

The idea came from the Babylonians about six thousand years ago. They thought that the sun revolved around the Earth in 360 days. Although they were wrong, because the Earth revolves around the sun and takes slightly more than 365 days, 360 is a very good number to divide a revolution into.

360 is a useful number because it has a lot of **factors**, that is numbers that divide exactly into it. The numbers 2, 3, 4, 5, 6, 8, 9, 10, 12 are all factors of 360; they all divide it exactly with no remainder.

● Can you find any more factors of 360?

Just as we have agreed to measure lengths in inches and can buy a ruler which is divided into inches, so we can buy a **protractor** for measuring angles. Rulers come in a 6-inch size and a 12-inch size. Protractors come in 180° – or 360° – sizes.

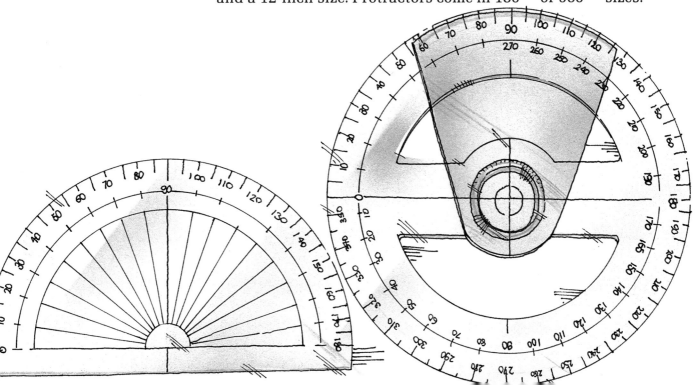

Folding Angles

1. Draw a circle. Either use a compass or draw around a circular object. The diameter needs to be about 4 to 5 inches so that you can fold the circle easily.

2. Cut out the circle carefully.

3. Fold it so that the edges match exactly. Do not open it up.

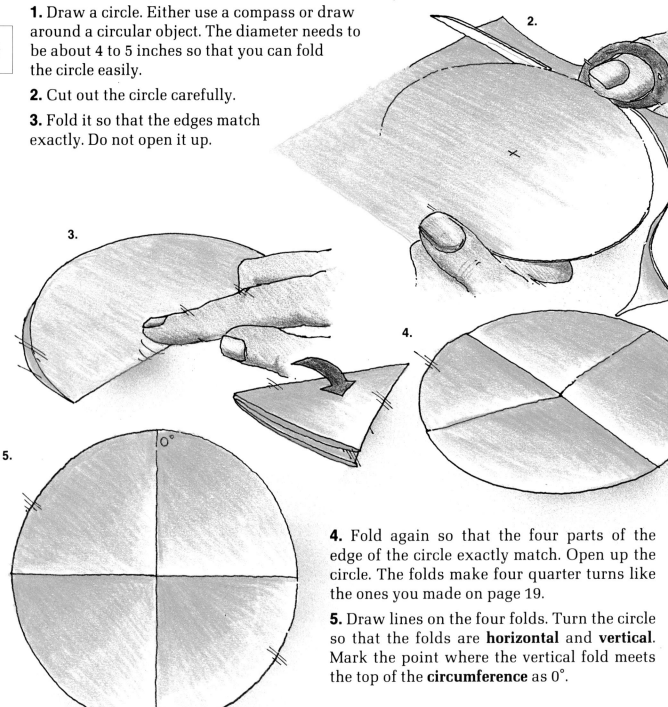

4. Fold again so that the four parts of the edge of the circle exactly match. Open up the circle. The folds make four quarter turns like the ones you made on page 19.

5. Draw lines on the four folds. Turn the circle so that the folds are **horizontal** and **vertical**. Mark the point where the vertical fold meets the top of the **circumference** as 0°.

6. With your finger, trace all around the circumference of the circle back to 0°. Your finger has made a whole turn, one revolution of 360°. Both 0° and 360° occupy the same point on the circumference of the circle.

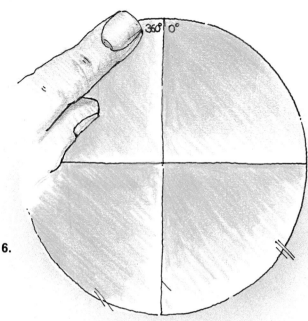

6.

7. With your finger, trace around the circumference to the bottom of the vertical fold. How much of a turn has your finger made? How many degrees has it turned? Mark the correct number of degrees on your circle.

8. With your finger, trace clockwise around the circumference from 0° to the first position where the horizontal fold meets the circumference. How much of a turn has your finger made? How many degrees has it turned? Mark the correct number of degrees on your circle.

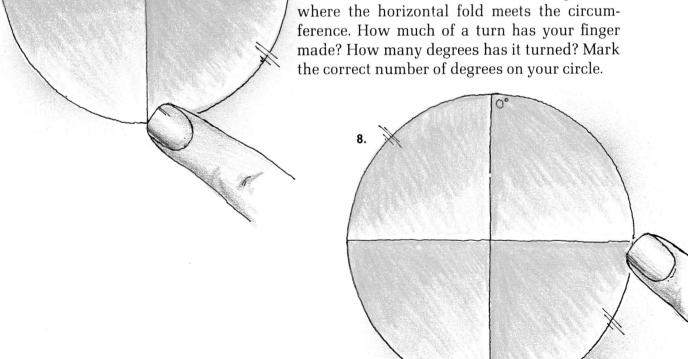

7.

8.

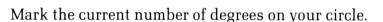

● **9.** With your finger, trace clockwise from 0° to the second position where the horizontal fold meets the circumference. How much of a turn has your finger made? How many degrees has it turned?

Mark the current number of degrees on your circle.

9.

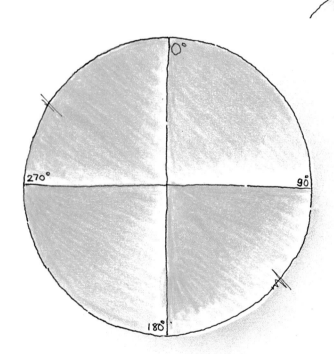

Your circle should now look like this.

A half turn = 180°. A quarter turn = 90°.

A three-quarter turn = 270°.

10.

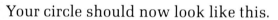

10. Refold your circle along the fold lines. Carefully fold it in half again.

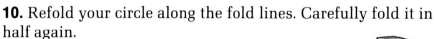

Open up the circle. Draw in the two new fold lines.

- **1.** How many equal parts is the circle divided into now?
- **2.** What fraction of a turn is each part?
- **3.** Write in the correct number of degrees in the four new positions on the circumference.

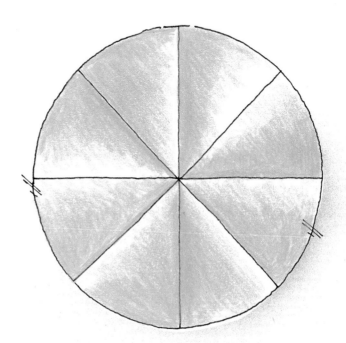

KEEP YOUR CIRCLE.

Around the Clock

● A minute hand on a clock makes one revolution in an hour. What fraction of a turn does the hour hand make in one hour? How many degrees does the hour hand turn in one hour?

26

Lay your paper circle in the middle of the drawing of the clock face on the opposite page. Position it so that the centers match, the 0° mark of your circle is in line with 12 o'clock, and the 180° mark of the circle is in line with the 6 o'clock. Use a ruler to check the position.

Use a ruler to transfer the marks for $\frac{1}{12}$ of a turn from the clock face to your paper circle.

Place the edge of the ruler on 7 and 1 o'clock and the center of the paper circle. Make two marks on the circumference of the paper circle. Repeat for the 2 and 8, 4 and 10 and 5 and 11 o'clock marks.

Be careful to keep the paper in position.

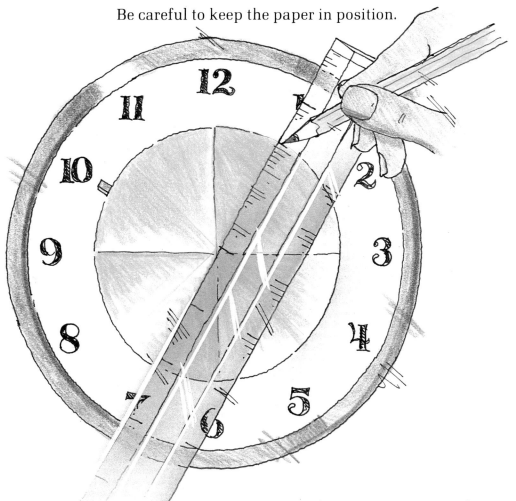

You now have eight new marks on your paper circle

● Write on the circle the number of degrees for each new mark.

Answers to page 26

The hour hand turns $\frac{1}{12}$ of a revolution in an hour. The hour hand turns 30° in an hour.

Answer to page 27

Your circle should look like this. Check that you have gotten the numbers right.

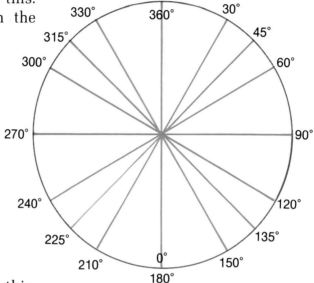

◇ Divide your circle up like this. Color the different **sectors** and cut them out carefully.

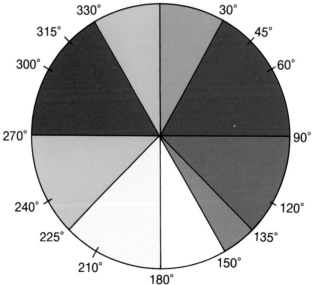

- **1.** How many degrees are left in the uncolored sector?
- **2.** Arrange the angles in order of size.

Degrees in a Right Angle

● How many different ways can you combine your sectors so that they total 90°?

Draw a diagram for each one like this.

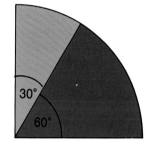

right angle sign

Another word for a quarter turn is a **right angle**.
A right angle has 90°.

◇ Look at your diagrams. Notice that each group of angles that adds up to 90° makes a quarter turn.

Right angles are marked with a box instead of the ordinary angle curve.

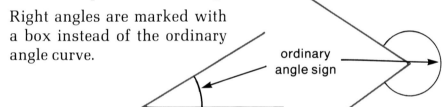

ordinary angle sign

If you look around, you can see that we use right angles all the time. See how many you can count in a day. A goal of one hundred will be no problem.

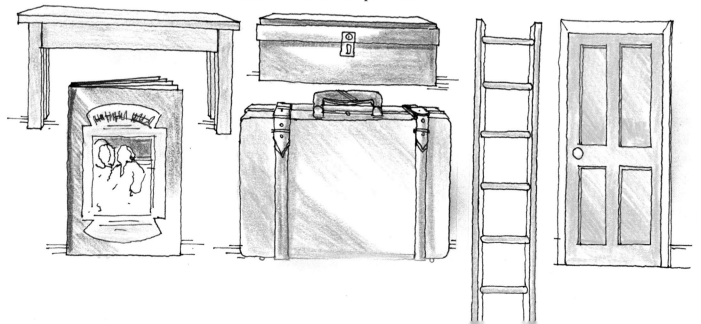

Two right angles make a straight line. This makes boxes and packages with right angles easy to pack together. They fit together to make straight lines and do not waste space. This is one reason that right angles are so commonly used. Some people do like living in curved houses but it is more difficult to fit in the furniture.

Next time you go shopping, look at the shapes of the packages that you buy. Most of the dry goods will be in boxes made of squares or rectangles with right angles.

● Look at the way cans are made. Most of them, especially those that contain liquid, are made with curved sides and do not have right angles. Can you think of any reasons for this?

A path made of square or rectangular slabs fits together and is easy to lay. If you use **pentagon** slabs you get gaps.

● Can you think of other shaped slabs that fit together with no gaps?

Degrees on a Straight Line

● **1.** How many different ways can you make 180° using the sectors of your circle? Draw a diagram of each way of doing it.

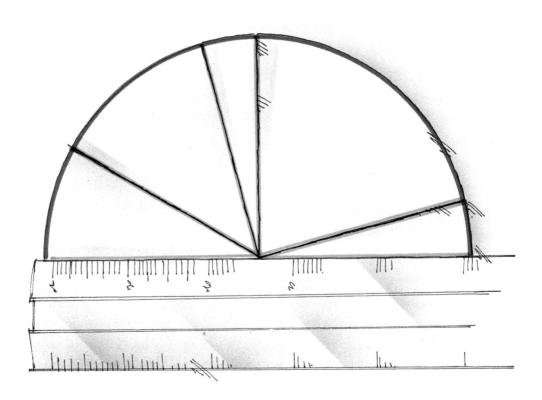

● **2.** Lay the edge of your ruler along each of the angles of 180° that you made. What do you notice?

● What is the missing angle in each of these pairs?

Calculate them; do not try to measure them. The first one is done for you.

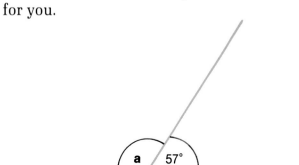

$a + 57° = 180°$ (a straight line)
$a = 180° - 57° = 123°$

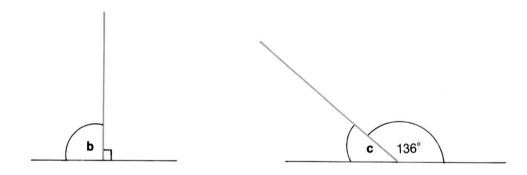

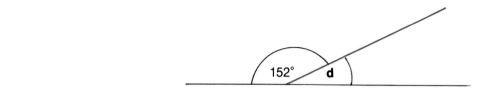

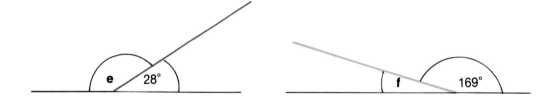

● Match your circle sectors to these wedges of cheese so that you can state the size of each angle that is marked.

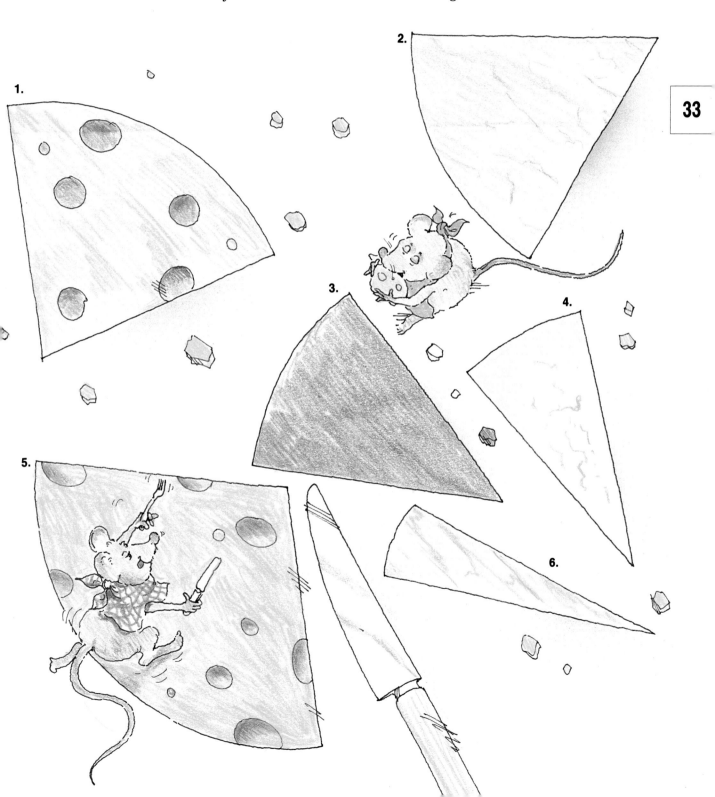

Estimating Angles

● Look carefully at these angles. Estimate the size of each of
them in degrees.

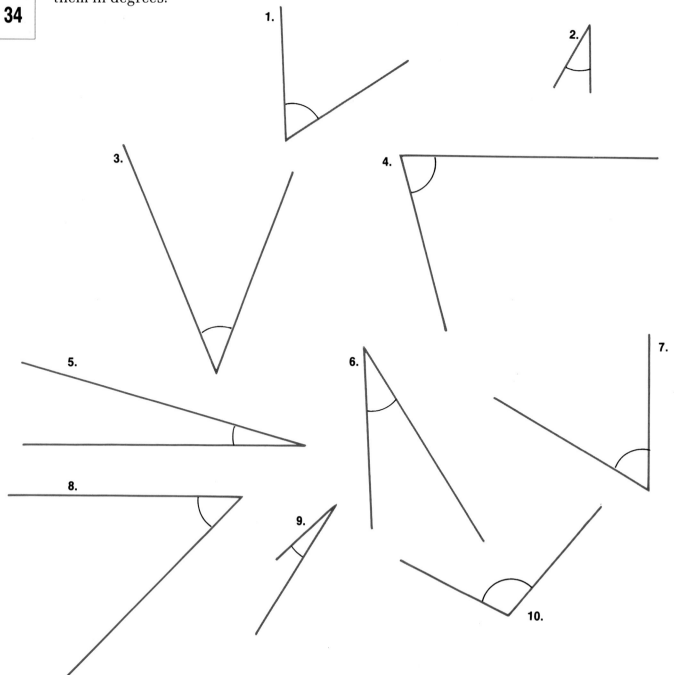

◇ Use a pencil and ruler to draw angles of:

1. 90°

2. 180°

3. 45°

4. 60°

5. 30°

6. 15°

7. 75°

8. 105°

9. 135°

10. 150°

◇ Use your circle sectors to see whether you have made the angles too small, too large or just right.

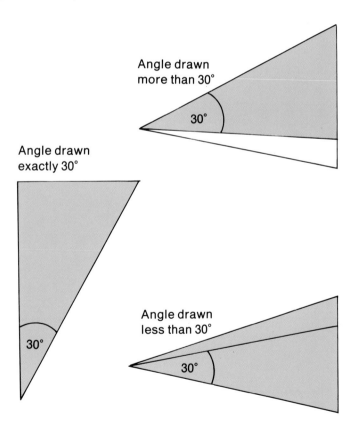

Angle drawn more than 30°

30°

Angle drawn exactly 30°

30°

Angle drawn less than 30°

30°

Measuring Angles with a Protractor

36

A protractor can help you to measure angles accurately in degrees. It is best to use a store—bought plastic, metal or wooden protractor. They are more accurately made than one you draw yourself.

If you are unable to buy a protractor, then use tracing paper to copy the one below. Be sure to trace it exactly.

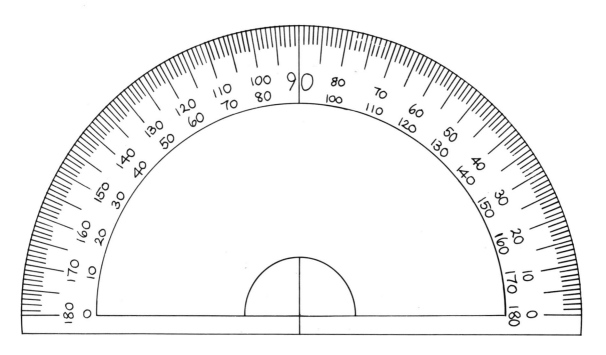

◇ Look at the numbers on the protractor. You can see that there are two sets. They each begin at 0° and end at 180°. One reads clockwise; the other reads counter-clockwise. when you are measuring an angle it does not matter which set of numbers you use but you must not change your mind half way around.

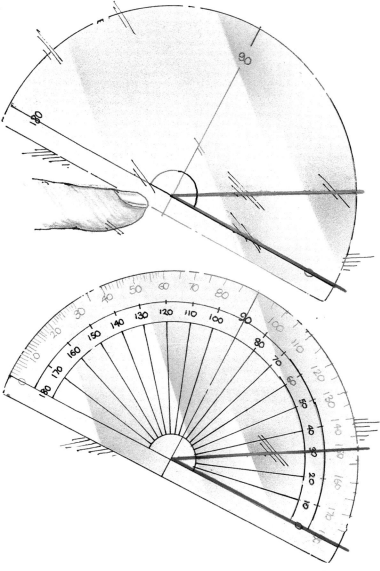

To measure an angle, first position the protractor over it so that the 0° to 180° line is on one of the arms of the angle. The point where the 90° line meets the 0° to 180° line must be on the **vertex** of the angle.

To measure this angle, you need to start from 0°, so use the inner scale. Count around from 0° until you reach the point on the inner scale that coincides with the second arm of the angle. Read off from the inner scale that the angle measures 30°.

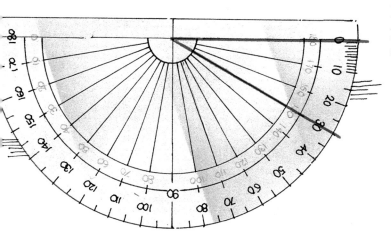

If you prefer to use the outside scale, you must use the protractor this way around.

Always look at the angle and make sure your answer makes sense. Is the angle less than a right angle, that is less than 90°? If it is more than a right angle, is it less than a straight line, that is less than 180°? This way you will notice if you have made a mistake and read the wrong scale.

If you are using a 360° protractor, place the center of the protractor on the vertex of the angle. Place 0° on one of the arms of the angle and read around the correct scale to the other arm of the angle.

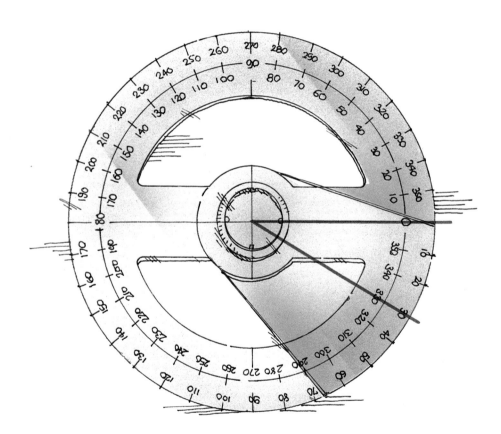

● Use a protractor to measure these angles which are marked in black. Record your answers.

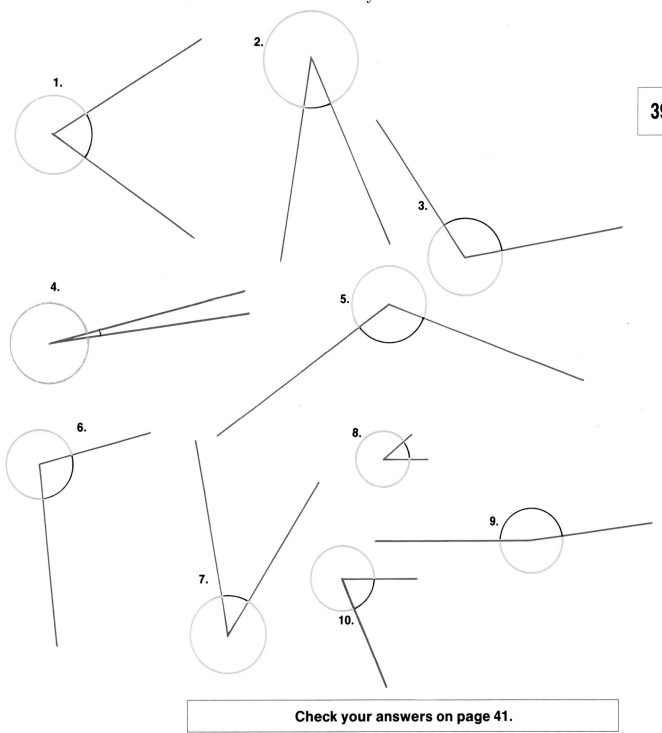

Check your answers on page 41.

Measuring angles greater than 180°

If you use a 360° protractor, you can easily measure an angle greater than 180°.

40

If you are using a 180° protractor, you can measure the angle in two stages.

1. Position your protractor as usual. Make a mark at the 180° line.

2. Remove the protractor and replace it as shown.

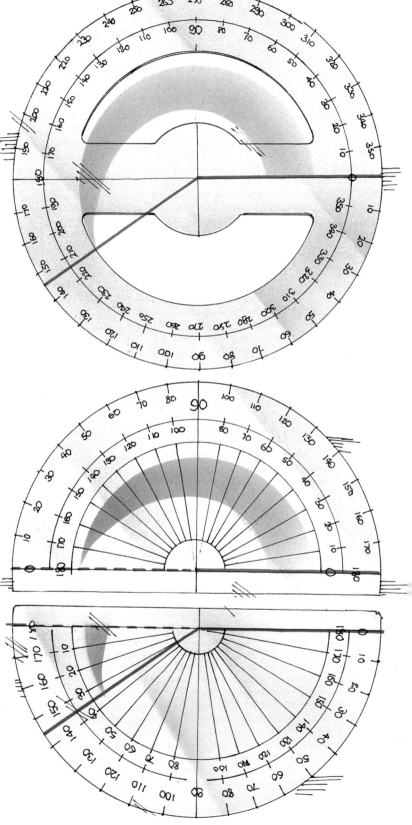

Read the angle. In this case it is 35°. Add 35° to the 180° you have already measured in stage **1**.
The angle measures $35° + 180° = 215°$.

There is no need for the first step once you are sure of yourself. Place the protractor in the step **2** position right away. But you must remember that you need to add 180° to whatever angle you measure when you use the protractor this way.

Investigation

- **A.** Measure the angles marked in blue on page 39.
- **B.** Total the inner and outer pair of angles in each example.
- What do you notice?
- Can you explain why it happens?

Turn to page 42.

Answers to measuring angles on page 39
1. 67°
2. 32°
3. 113°
4. 6°
5. 123°
6. 99°
7. 41°
8. 40°
9. 172°
10. 67°

If your answers are the same or not more than 2° bigger or smaller than these, then count them as correct. If seven or more of your answers are correct, turn back to page 40.

If you got fewer than seven answers right, then go back and measure the angles again to see where you went wrong. When you are satisfied that you can use a protractor, then read page 40.

● Measure the marked angles in each of these drawings. Write down your results.

● Total each set. Write down what you think the remaining blue shaded angle in each drawing will measure.

● Measure it to see if you are correct.

42

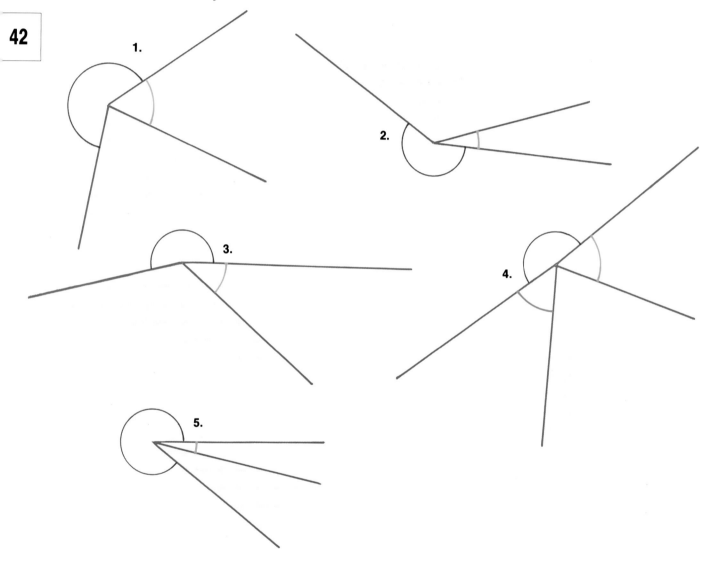

● What have you found out about angles that meet around a point?

Check your answers on page 63 before you continue.

Calculating Angles

Calculate the missing angle in these drawings. *Do not try to measure them.* Use what you have found out about angles that meet around a point, angles that make a straight line and the number of degrees in a right angle.

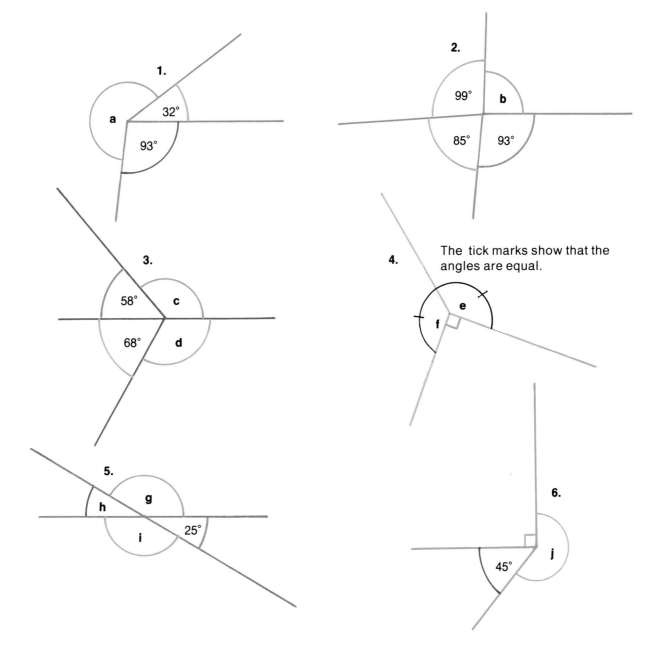

1. a, 32°, 93°

2. 99°, b, 85°, 93°

3. 58°, c, 68°, d

4. e, f — The tick marks show that the angles are equal.

5. h, g, i, 25°

6. j, 45°

Kinds of Angles

Angles are sorted according to size and given names.

44

Acute angles

Angles that are less than 90° are called **acute**. These are all acute angles.

Right angles

As you have already learned, angles of exactly 90° are called right angles.

Obtuse angles

Angles that are greater than 90° but less than 180° are called **obtuse** angles. These are all obtuse angles.

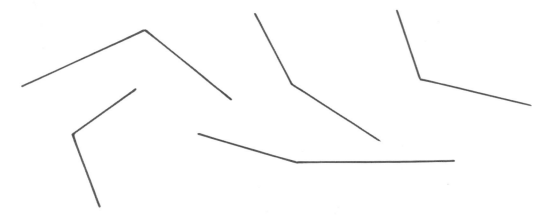

Reflex angles

Angles that are greater than 180° are called **reflex** angles. These are all reflex angles.

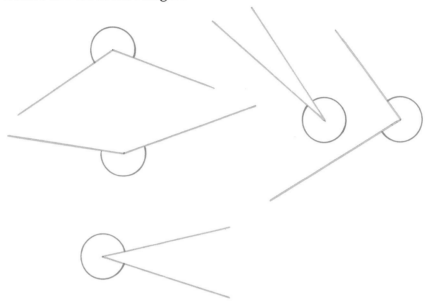

Inside and outside angles

Look again at the acute, right and obtuse angles. You can see that they each have a partner angle that is reflex.

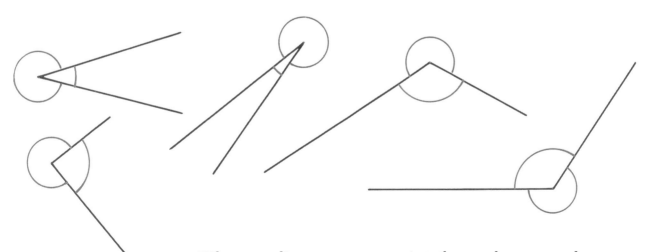

When two lines meet at a point, they make two angles – an inside angle and an outside angle. This is why it is important to mark the angle you are concerned with.

● Sort these angles into acute, right, obtuse and reflex angles.

46

Estimating Angles

47

● Write down your estimate (intelligent guess) of the size of each of these angles.

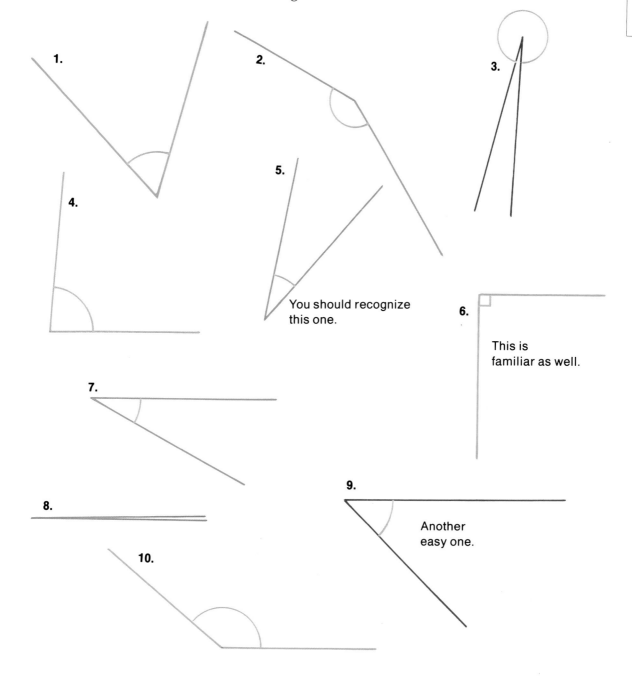

1.

2.

3.

4.

5.

You should recognize this one.

6.

This is familiar as well.

7.

8.

9.

Another easy one.

10.

Answers to page 47

The answers are: **1.** 59°, **2.** 150°, **3.** 348°, **4.** 85°, **5.** 30°, **6.** 90°, **7.** 28°, **8.** 1°, **9.** 45° and **10.** 140°.

If your estimate was not more than 2° bigger or smaller than the answer, then count it as correct.

◇ Try to draw these angles as accurately as you can, without a protractor. **1.** 30°, **2.** 50°, **3.** 127°, **4.** 290°, **5.** 325°, **6.** 3°, **7.** 90°, **8.** 185°, **9.** 15° and **10.** 135°.

◇ Check your drawings with a protractor. Count your answers as correct if you are within 2°.

◇ With a friend, try testing each other on drawing and estimating angles.

Perpendiculars

Perpendiculars are lines which are at right angles to each other. A **vertical** line and a **horizontal** line are perpendicular to each other. Builders use plumb lines and levels to ensure that their corners make exact right angles.

A plumb line is simply a piece of lead on the end of a string which hangs straight down. It is used to mark a vertical line.

A level is a glass tube nearly filled with liquid, usually set into a piece of wood or metal. When the level is held horizontal, the air bubble is exactly in the middle of the tube.

48

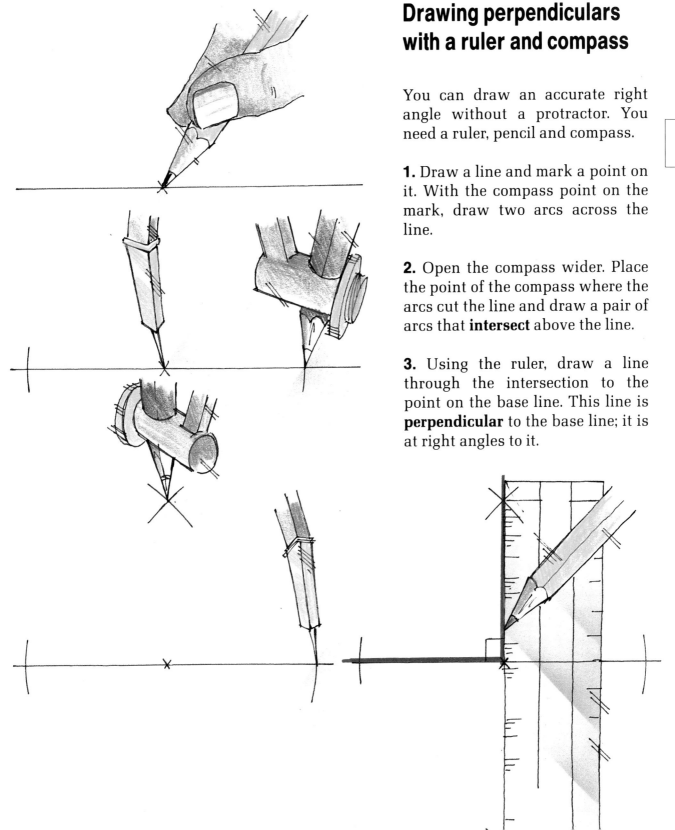

Drawing perpendiculars with a ruler and compass

You can draw an accurate right angle without a protractor. You need a ruler, pencil and compass.

1. Draw a line and mark a point on it. With the compass point on the mark, draw two arcs across the line.

2. Open the compass wider. Place the point of the compass where the arcs cut the line and draw a pair of arcs that **intersect** above the line.

3. Using the ruler, draw a line through the intersection to the point on the base line. This line is **perpendicular** to the base line; it is at right angles to it.

49

Bisecting an Angle

You can **bisect** an angle with a ruler and compass.

1. Draw the angle. Place the point of the compass on the vertex of the angle and make an arc on each arm of the angle.

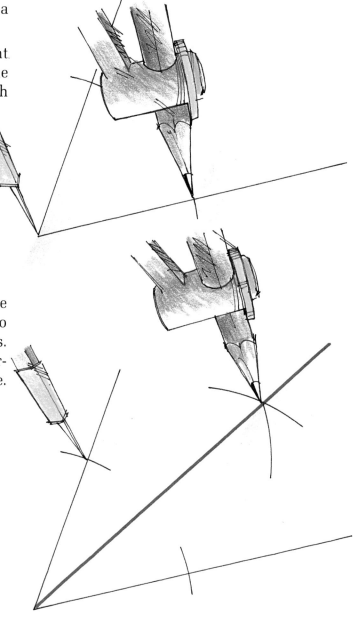

2. Open the compass wider. Place the point on each arc in turn to draw a pair of intersecting arcs. Draw a line from the point of inter-section to the vertex of the angle. This line bisects the angle.

An Angle Jigsaw

The heavy lines show the edges of the finished jigsaw. The four corners of the jigsaw are all right-angles.

● Make exact copies of these pieces. Arrange them to make a 5-inch square. If you use what you have learned about angles on a straight line, it should take you only a few minutes.

Angle Dominoes

You can also use the pieces from the angle jigsaw to play angle dominoes with a friend.

Divide up the pieces equally between the two of you. Take turns to lay down a piece, making a straight line each time. If you cannot make a straight line, you miss a turn. You are not allowed to overlap pieces. The player who is left with the fewest pieces is the winner.

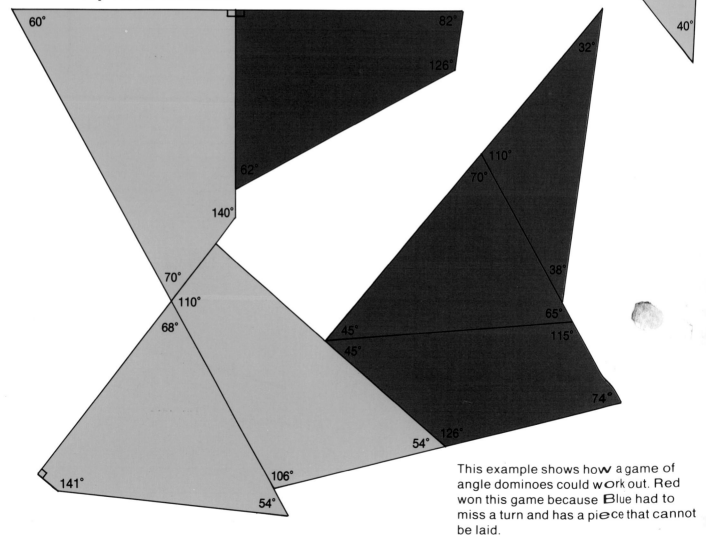

This example shows how a game of angle dominoes could work out. Red won this game because Blue had to miss a turn and has a piece that cannot be laid.

Making a Periscope

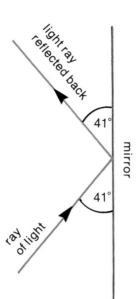

light ray
reflected back

41°

mirror

41°

ray
of light

When a ray of light hits a mirror at an angle it is reflected back from the mirror at the same angle.

You can use this property of light to make a simple periscope. A periscope is a device to allow you to see objects when your view is blocked by something else in front of you. You can use it to see over the heads of the people in front of you in a crowd.

A sophisticated version, using a series of lenses as well as two mirrors is used in submarines so that the crew can see ships on the surface when the submarine is submerged.

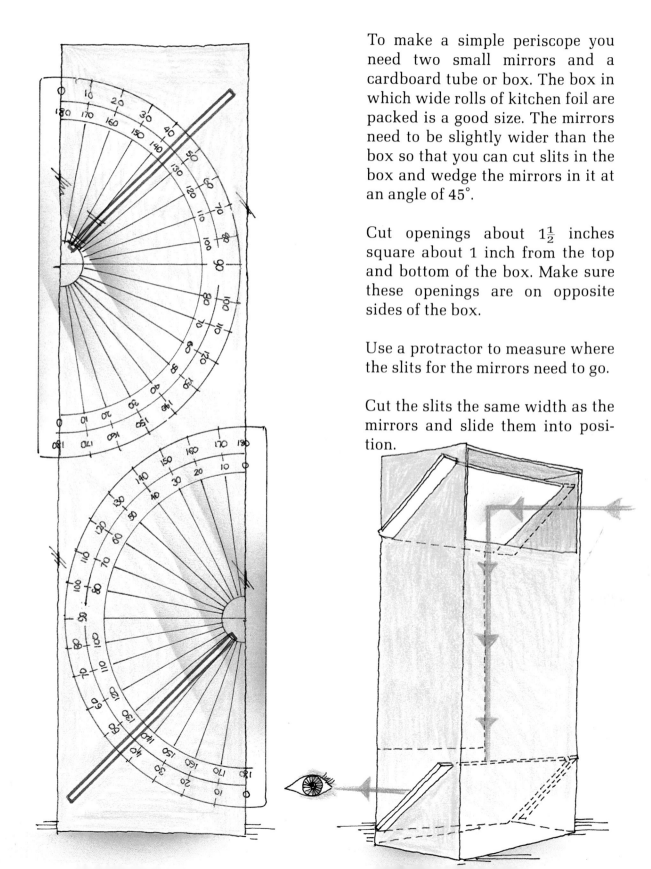

To make a simple periscope you need two small mirrors and a cardboard tube or box. The box in which wide rolls of kitchen foil are packed is a good size. The mirrors need to be slightly wider than the box so that you can cut slits in the box and wedge the mirrors in it at an angle of 45°.

Cut openings about $1\frac{1}{2}$ inches square about 1 inch from the top and bottom of the box. Make sure these openings are on opposite sides of the box.

Use a protractor to measure where the slits for the mirrors need to go.

Cut the slits the same width as the mirrors and slide them into position.

Similar Triangles

You have already seen that the length of the arms of an angle make no difference to the size of the angle.

● These angles are the same. What size do you estimate them to be?

A series of triangles have been drawn here which all share the same angle **a**.

$$\mathbf{a} = 26°$$
$$\tfrac{1}{2} \text{ base} = \text{height}$$

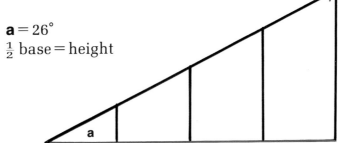

◇ Measure the length of the base and the height of each triangle. Copy the table below and record them as shown.

Base	Height	Height ÷ Base
1″	½″	½

● What do you notice?

Triangles with equal angles but unequal length sides are **similar**. Check that all the triangles in the diagram have equal angles.

Making a Clinometer

You can use the fact that similar triangles have equal angles to help you to measure the height of tall objects and buildings.

You need an instrument called a **clinometer**. If you cannot borrow a clinometer from school, you can make one.

Making a clinometer

You need:

A rectangular piece of cardboard 4 inches by 5 inches.
A straw or a pencil.
A protractor.
A piece of string 7 or 8 inches long.
A weight such as a nut and some adhesive tape.

Check that the four corners of your piece of cardboard are right angles using the protractor. Draw a line $\frac{1}{2}$ inch down from the top edge of the cardboard. Mark the center point of the line. Attach the straw to the cardboard in this space with adhesive tape.

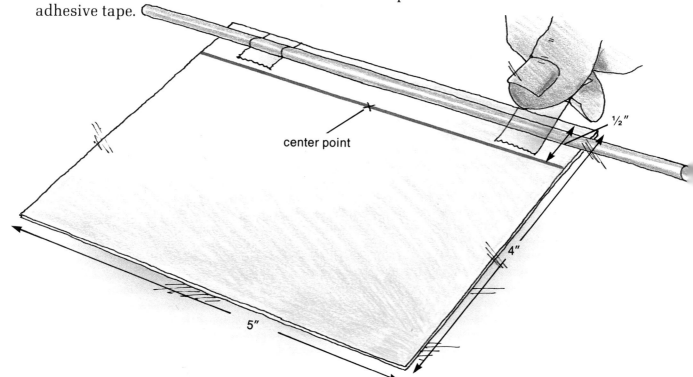

center point

½"

4"

5"

Place a protractor so that the 0° to 180° line is on the $\frac{1}{2}$ inch line and the 90° line is on the center point. Keep the protractor still and mark off every 5°.

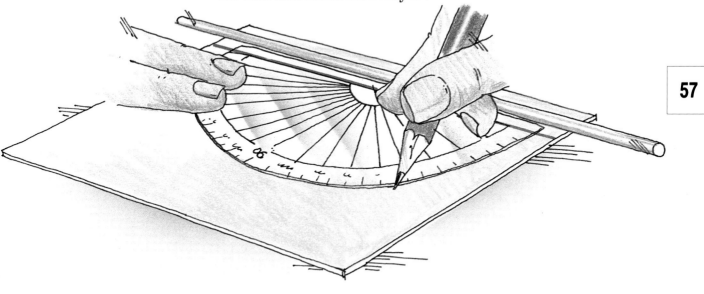

Mark the 90° line on the protractor as 0° on your clinometer. Write in each 10° on each side until you get back to 0° on each side.

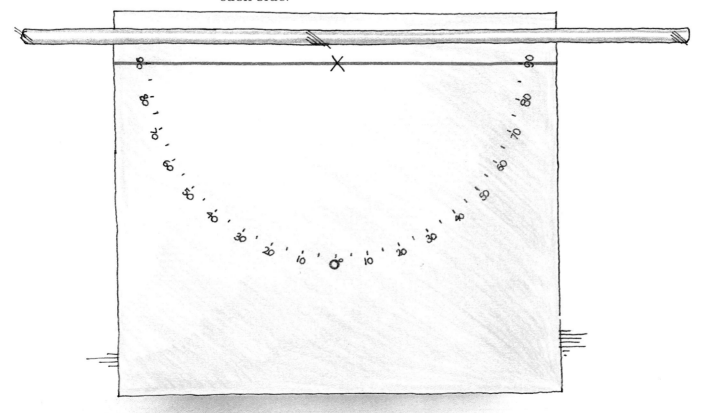

Tie the nut to the string. Place the string on the center point of the line so that it hangs down on the 0° line. Attach it securely at the back of the cardboard with adhesive tape.

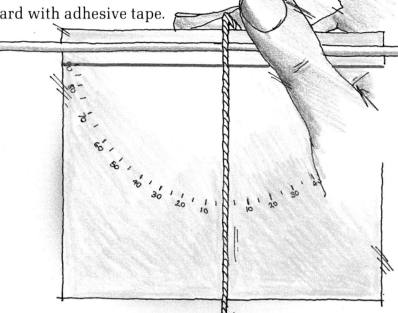

Tilt the cardboard up and down to check that the string hangs freely on both sides of 0°.

To use the clinometer, point the straw at the top of the building you wish to measure. Look along the straw and make sure it is pointing as exactly at the top as you can get it. If possible, have someone to read off for you the angle that the string is on. If you have to do it yourself, hold the string with your thumb when you have gotten the straw in the right position and then look at the angle afterward.

You have only marked off the angles every 5°, so you will have to estimate the angle to the nearest degree.

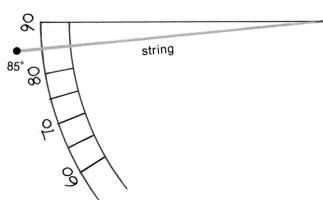

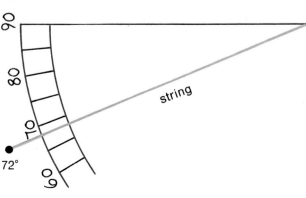

Measuring the Height of a Tall Building

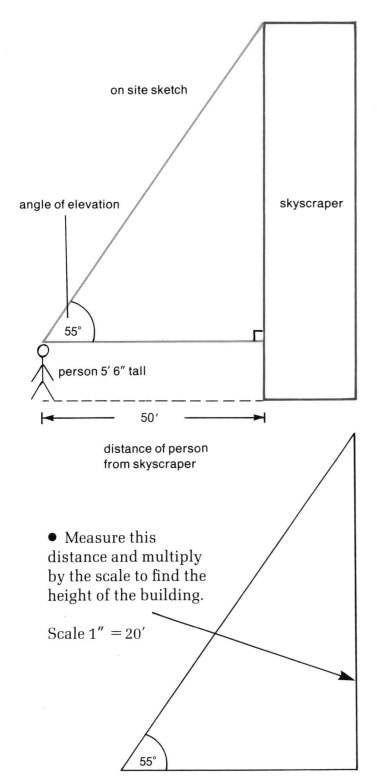

on site sketch

skyscraper

angle of elevation

55°

person 5′ 6″ tall

50′

distance of person
from skyscraper

● Measure this
distance and multiply
by the scale to find the
height of the building.

Scale 1″ = 20′

55°

Go and stand where you can see the top of the building. Measure the **angle of elevation** of the building with a **clinometer**. Measure your height and the horizontal distance from you to the building.

Draw a sketch of the building, the distance it is viewed from and the angle of elevation. This makes a right-angled triangle. Write in the measurements.

Go to a desk and make an accurate scale drawing of your triangle. You need to choose a sensible scale. In the example, a scale of 1″ : 20′ (1 inch in the drawing equals 20 actual feet) has been used. Remember to state your scale on the drawing.

Be as careful and precise as you can in your measuring and scale drawing to get an accurate result. Note that you must add your height to the result.

Glossary

acute   an acute angle is less than 90°

angle of elevation   the angle between the horizontal and the line from an observer to an object above

bisect   to divide in half. You can bisect a line or an angle.

circumference   the distance, or the line, around the edge of a circle

clinometer   an instrument for measuring angles of elevation

factor   a factor divides a number exactly with no remainder

horizontal   at right angles to an upright, or vertical, line. The horizon appears to be a horizontal straight line. (It is actually curved because the Earth is a sphere.)

intersect   lines which meet or cross at one point intersect each other

obtuse   an obtuse angle is greater than 90° and less than 180°

pentagon   a closed shape with five straight sides

perpendicular   two lines are perpendicular when they meet at right angles

protractor   an instrument for measuring angles

reflex   a reflex angle is greater than 180°

revolution   one complete turn

right angle   an angle of 90°; a quarter turn

sector   a wedge cut from a curved shape

similar   similar shapes have the same proportion but are not the same size

vertex   the point where two lines meet to form an angle

vertical   an upright line at right angles to the horizontal

Answers

Page 7
See page 8
Page 8
See page 10
Page 9
1. One whole turn
2. Five whole turns
3. Two whole turns
Pages 10-12
See page 14
Page 13
The words are:
BEAD and FACE.
The drawings for CAB are like this

Pages 14-15
1. Yes, it is always a quarter turn.
2. A quarter turn
3. A half turn
4. A half turn
5. A half turn
Page 17
See page 18
Page 18
See page 20
Page 19
The angles that are more than a quarter turn
are: **1,2** and **6**. Angles **3** and **4** are less than a
quarter turn. **5** is exactly a quarter turn.

Page 20
1. They are all the same; the length of the lines makes no difference to the size of the angle.
2. There are 16 quarter turns in **a**, 3 in **b** and 7 in **c**.

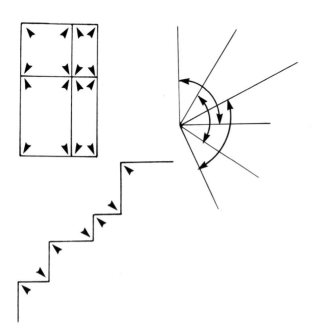

Page 21
15, 18, 24, 30, 36, 40, 45, 60, 72, 90, 120 and 180 are all factors of 360.

Page 23
7. Your finger has made half a turn. It has turned 180°.
8. Your finger has made a quarter of a turn. It has turned 90°.

Page 24
9. Your finger has made three-quarters of a turn. It has turned 270°.

Page 25
1. The circle is divided into eight equal parts.
2. Each part is one eighth of a turn.
3. 45°, 135°, 225°, 315°

Page 26
See page 28

Page 27
See page 28

Page 28
1. 30° are in the uncolored sector.
2. 15°, 30°, 45°, 60°, 75°, 105°.

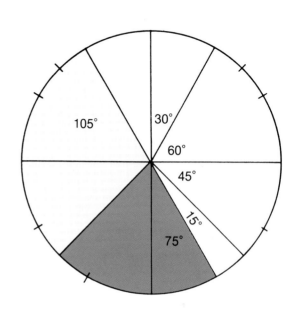

Page 29
Ways of making 90° with the sectors: 30° and 60°; 30°, 45° and 15°; 75° and 15°.

Page 30
Sharp edges are more likely to get dented. Cylinders can be made with only one seam down the side, or with none.
Triangular, quadrilateral and hexagonal slabs will all fit together with no gaps.

Page 31
1. Ways of making 180° with the sectors: 30°, 30°, 60°; 45° and 15°; 30°, 60°, 75° and 15°; 105° and 75°; 105°, 60° and 15°; 105°, 30° and 45°; 105°, 30°, 30° and 15°.
2. Angles that add up to 180° make a straight line.

Page 32
a) $180° - 57° = 123°$, **b)** $180° - 90° = 90°$,
c) $180° - 136° = 44°$ **d)** $180° - 152° = 28°$
e) $180° - 28° = 152°$ **f)** $180° - 169° = 11°$

Page 33
1. $75°$ **2.** $60°$ **3.** $45°$ **4.** $30°$ **5.** $105°$ **6.** $15°$

Page 34
1. $60°$ **2.** $30°$ **3.** $45°$ **4.** $75°$ **5.** $15°$ **6.** $30°$ **7.** $60°$
8. $45°$ **9.** $15°$ **10.** $105°$

Page 41
A. 1. $293°$
　　2. $328°$
　　3. $247°$
　　4. $354°$
　　5. $237°$
　　6. $261°$
　　7. $319°$
　　8. $320°$
　　9. $188°$
　　10. $293°$

B. Each pair of angles totals $360°$ because together they make a complete turn.

Page 42
1. $360° - (58° + 225°) = 360° - 283° = 77°$
2. $360° - (210° + 21°) = 360° - 231° = 129°$
3. $360° - (194° + 40°) = 360° - 234° = 126°$
4. $360° - (59° + 177° + 50°) = 360° - 286° = 74°$
5. $360° - (13° + 322°) = 360° - 335° = 25°$
Angles that meet around a point total $360°$.

Page 43
1.
$a = 360° - (32° + 93°) = 360° - 125° = 235°$
2.
$b = 360° - (99° + 85° + 93°) = 360° - 277° = 83°$
3.
$c = 180° - 58° = 122°$, $d = 180° - 68° = 112°$
4.
$e + f = 360° - 90° = 270°$, $270° \div 2 = 135° =$
$e = f$

5.
$g = 180° - 25° = 155°$, $h = 180° - g = 25°$
$i = 180° - 25° = 155°$
6.
$j = 360° - (90° + 45°) = 360° - 135° = 225°$

Page 46
Acute: **a c, g, i, l, o, p**
Right: **d, e, f**
Obtuse: **b, h, k, n, q, m**
Reflex: **j** and **n**

Page 47
See page 48

Page 51

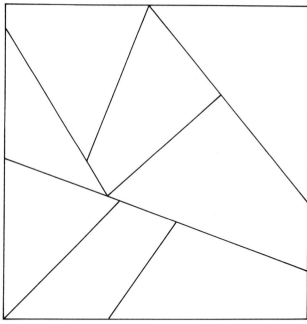

Page 55
The angles are both $10°$.
The height is always half the base. The triangles are all in the same proportion.

Page 59
It measures $3\frac{1}{2}''$. The building must be $70'$ tall. Remember to add $5'\ 6''$ for the height of the viewer.
Total height of the building $= 75'\ 6''$.

Index